QUOTE UNQUOTE

Latin

QUOTE UNQUOTE

Latin

Edited by
ANTHONY LEJEUNE

STACEY
INTERNATIONAL

Stacey International
128 Kensington Church Street
London W8 4BH
Telephone: +44 (0)20 7221 7166 Fax: +44 (0)20 7792 9288
Email: info@stacey-international.co.uk
www.stacey-international.co.uk

First published by Stacey International in 1998
as part of *The Concise Dictionary of Foreign Quotations*

© Stacey International 2008

ISBN: 978-1-9052-9959-1

Series editor: Anthony Lejeune
Assistant editor: Kitty Carruthers

British Library Cataloguing-in-Publication Data
A catalogue record for this publication is available
from the British Library

FOREWORD

'Classical quotation,' said Dr Johnson, 'is the *parole* of literary men all over the world.' And not just literary men. Until quite recently even politicians could toss Latin quotations at each other across the floor of the Commons. Every schoolboy really did know that Caesar divided all Gaul into three parts. Every educated Englishman, certainly every educated Scotsman, had a few tags from Horace, Ovid or Virgil up his sleeve. Those three Roman poets were, apart from the Bible and Shakespeare, probably the most quoted in Western Europe.

Latin is a language particularly well suited for producing quotable quotes, being lapidary like a mosaic, with grammatical parts which fit neatly together forming ideas which would take far more words to express in English.

Many of the quotations and phrases in this little book remain at least vaguely familiar. 'Alma mater', for example, 'Habeas corpus' and 'Decus et tutamen' which is inscribed on every English pound coin. There are legal terms – 'Sub judice' and 'Caveat emptor'; ecclesiastical – 'Nunc dimittis', 'Mea culpa' and the Pope's blessing, 'Urbi et orbi'; philosophic or logical – 'Reductio ad absurdum', 'Sine qua non', 'Post hoc, ergo propter hoc'; all much clearer and more concise in Latin than in English.

There are some which are easy to translate and some – 'Sunt lacrimæ rerum' or 'Simplex munditiis' – which, notoriously, are almost impossible to convey. And there are one or two which, while not familiar, seemed irresistible, such as 'Emax domina', recognisable down the ages – 'The lady is addicted to shopping'.

So, whether to refresh dimly remembered knowledge or as an introduction to new pearls, this book is a small treasure chest. Read, contemplate and chuckle. Impress your friends by quoting Caesar and Cicero. Annoy your opponents by quoting them in Latin.

Anthony Lejeune
September 2007

Thomas à Kempis (c 1380-1471)
Homo proponit, sed Deus disponit.
Man proposes but God disposes.

Peter Abelard (1079-1142)
O quanta qualia sunt illa sabbata
Quae semper celebrat superna curia.
O what sabbaths, and how many, are those which the
company of heaven perpetually enjoys.

Alciatus (1492-1550)
Bis dat qui cito dat.
He gives twice who gives quickly.

Consuetudo vicit: quae cum omnium domina rerum, tum
maxime verborum est.
Usage won: usage which rules all things and especially
language.

Alcuin (735-804)
Nec audiendi qui solent dicere, Vox populi, vox Dei, quum
tumultuositas vulgi semper insaniae proxima sit.
They should not be listened to who keep saying that
'The voice of the people is the voice of God', since
the turbulence of the crowd is always very near to
madness.

St Ambrose (339-397)
Credo ut intelligam.
I believe in order that I may understand.

Te Deum laudamus.

We praise thee, O Lord.
> *Hymn, said to have been improvised by St Ambrose while baptising St Augustine*

Anon

Absit omen.
May it not be an omen.
> *Latin expression*

Aegrot at daemon, monachus tunc esse volebat;
Daemon convaluit, daemon ut ante fuit.
The devil was sick, the devil a monk would be; the devil got well, the devil a monk was he.
> *Mediaeval saying*

Afflavit Deus et dissipantur.
God blew and they were scattered.
> *Queen Elizabeth's medal, commemorating the destruction of the Spanish Armada*

Alma mater.
The mother who nurtured us.
> *Roman expression*

Ars est celare artem.
Art consists in concealing the art.
> *Roman maxim*

Ars gratia artis.
Art for art's sake.
> *Adoped as the motto of Metro-Goldwyn-Mayer*

Ave, Caesar, morituri te salutant
Hail, Caesar. Those who are about to die salute thee!
Gladiators' salute on entering the arena

Brutum fulmen.
Mindless lightning (*i.e.* a loud but harmless outburst).
Latin expression

Catus amat pisces sed non vult tingere plantas.
The cat loves fish but doesn't want to get his feet wet.
Mediaeval adage

Cetera desunt.
The rest is missing.
Copyists' or scholars' expression

Ceteris paribus.
Other things being equal.
Latin expression

Corruptio optimi pessima.
The best when corrupted becomes the worst.
Latin saying

Cucullus non facit monachum.
The cowl does not make the monk.
Mediaeval saying

Cum grano salis.
With a grain of salt.
(*Because we'd need salt to help us swallow it.*)
Roman expression

Currente calamo.
With a flowing pen.
> *Roman expression*

De gustibus non disputandum.
There's no arguing about tastes.
> *Mediaeval scholiasts' saying*

De mortuis nil nisi bonum.
One should speak only good of the dead.
> *Latin saying, adapted from the Greek sage Chilon*

Divide et impera.
Divide and rule.
> *Roman maxim*

Dum spiro, spero.
While I breathe, I hope.
> *Motto*

Dum vivimus, vivamus.
While we live, let us live.
> *From an ancient inscription*

Et ego in Arcadia or *Et in Arcadia ego.*
Either 'I too have lived in Arcady,' or 'Even in Arcady
there am I.'
> *Latin phrase*

Ex pede Herculem.
You can tell the size of Hercules from his footprint. (6ft 7ins, according to Pythagoras, who worked it out from the Olympic stadium which had supposedly been measured by the hero's foot.)
  Latin saying

Exeunt omnes.
They all go out.
  Stage direction

Experto crede Roberto.
Trust Robert; he's been there.
  Mediaeval maxim.

Fiat experimentum in corpore vili.
Let the experiment be made on a worthless body.
  Latin saying

Floreat Etona.
May Eton flourish.
  Eton College motto

Fons et origo.
The fountain and source.
  Latin expression

Functus officio.
Having discharged his duties.
  Latin expression, of an official whose task has been completed

Gaudeamus igitur
Iuvenes dum sumus.
Post iucundam iuventutem,
Post molestam senectutem,
Nos habebit humus.
Then let us rejoice while we are young. After sweet
youth, after burdensome age, the earth will hold us.
  Mediaeval students' song

Genius loci.
The genius [presiding spirit] of the place.
  Latin expression

Graecum est. Non potest legi.
This is Greek. Impossible to read.
  Mediaeval scribes

Horas non numero nisi serenas.
I count only the sunny hours.
  Inscription on sundials

Ignorantia elenchi.
Missing the point of the argument.
  Logicians' term

Ignotum per ignotius.
To explain something not understood by something
even less understood.
  Latin expression

In hoc signo vinces.
By this sign shalt thou conquer.
> *Words seen by the Emperor Constantine, accompanying a cross in the sky*

In loco parentis.
In place of a parent.
> *Latin phrase, often of schoolteachers*

In statu pupillari.
In the rank or condition of a pupil.
> *University statutes describing undergraduates*

Infra dignitatem.
Beneath one's dignity.
> *Latin phrase, usually just 'Infra dig'*

Inter alia.
Among other things.
> *Latin expression*

Inter pocula.
Between drinks.
> *Latin expression*

Ipsissima verba.
The actual words.
> *Latin expression*

Ius primae noctis.
A claim to the first night (with a newly married bride).
> *Mediaeval expression, of a feudal lord's supposed entitlement*

Lapsus calami.
A slip of the pen.
   Latin phrase

Lares et penates.
Household gods, guardians of hearth and home.
   Roman phrase

Literae humaniores.
Humane letters, the humanities.
   Academic phrase; at Oxford the study of the classics,
   ancient history and philosophy

Magna civitas, magna solitudo.
A great city, a great loneliness.
   Latin translation of a line from Greek comedy

Malo malo malo malo.
Malo, I would rather be,
Malo, in an apple tree,
Malo, than a naughty boy,
Malo, in adversity.
   Schoolboy joke playing on the different meanings of what
   looks like the same word

Me iudice.
In my opinion.
   Latin expression

Memento mori.
Remember thou wilt die.
> *Philosophic or theological injunction represented by a*
> *sobering object or warning*

Modus vivendi.
A way of living.
> *Latin expression, especially of adverse parties learning to*
> *live together*

More maiorum.
In the manner of our fathers.
> *Latin phrase*

Multum in parvo.
Much contained in a small compass.
> *Latin expression*

Nemo me impune lacessit.
No one provokes me unpunished.
> *Latin motto; the motto in the Royal Arms for Scotland, used*
> *by the Order of the Thistle*

Nihil simile est idem.
Things similar are not identical
> *Latin proposition*

Non compos mentis.
Off his head (*i.e.* mad).
> *Latin phrase*

Novus homo.
A new man (*i.e.* an upstart)
> *Roman expression*

Obiter dictum.
Something said incidentally.
> *Latin phrase*

Odium scholasticum or *Odium theologicum.*
Hatred between scholars or between theologians.
> *Mediaeval expression*

Per ardua ad astra.
With endurance to the stars.
> *Motto of the Royal Air Force*

Petitio principii.
Begging the question.
> *Logical fallacy, assuming as a premise the conclusion to be proved*

Pollice verso.
Thumbs down.
> *signal given in the arena when one gladiator was at the mercy of another*

Posse comitatus.
A posse.
> *Mediaeval Latin for the assembly summoned to help the sheriff*

Post hoc, ergo propter hoc.
After this, therefore because of this.
> *Logical fallacy*

Primus inter pares.
First among equals.
> *Latin phrase, e.g. the Prime Minister's position in the Cabinet*

Quantum sufficit.
As much as necessary.
> *Medical term, often simply 'quant.suff.'*

Quidquid agis, prudenter agis et respice finem.
Whatever you do, do prudently and look to the end.
> *Gesta Romanorum*

Quod erat demonstrandum.
Which was to be demonstrated.
> *Geometry book, usually just 'QED'*

Reductio ad absurdum.
Reduction to absurdity.
> *Logicians' phrase, demonstrating, by carrying it to extremes, the absurdity of an opponent's position*

Relata refero.
I tell what I've been told.
> *Latin phrase*

Saeva indignatio.
Fierce indignation.
> Jonathan Swift's epitaph (*Ubi saeva indignatio ulterius cor lacerare nequit.*)

Sal Atticum.
Attic salt (*i.e.* wit).
> *Roman expression*

Sardonius risus.
A sardonic smile.
> *Roman expression, referring to a bitter herb which grew in Sardinia and contorted the features of those who tasted it.*

Si monumentum requiris, circumspice.
If you seek him monument, look around you.
> *Sir Christopher Wren's memorial in St Paul's Cathedral*

Sine qua non.
Without which, not (*i.e.* indispensable).
> *Latin expression*

Solamen miseris socios habuisse doloris.
Having companions in sorrow is a comfort to the wretched.
> *Mephosophilis in Marlowe's Dr Faustus*

Solvitur ambulando.
The question is solved as we proceed.
> *Philosophers' phrase*

Sortes Virgilianae.
The Virgilian lottery (i.e. opening Virgil at random, as some Christians open the Bible, seeking an oracle).
Latin phrase

SPQR: Senatus Populusque Romanus.
The Senate and the People of Rome.
Initials inscribed on military standards

Status quo ante bellum.
The situation before war began (e.g. to restore it).
Latin phrase used mainly about international affairs

Stet.
Let it stand (i.e. ignore deletion or correction).
Instruction to printers

Suaviter in modo, fortiter in re.
Gentle in manner, strong in practice.
Latin motto, adopted by the Jesuits

Sub rosa.
Under the rose (i.e. under a seal of silence).
Because Cupid once bribed Harpocrates, the god of Silence, with a rose not to divulge the amours of Venus, a rose hanging above the table became a symbol of discretion.
Latin expression

Suggestio falsi, suppression veri.
False implications, suppression of the truth.
Latin phrases for statements which, though not actually untruthful, are deliberately misleading

13

Sui generis.
Of its own special kind, unique.
> *Latin phrase*

Suspirium puellarum.
The love-sigh of girls.
> *Graffiti found in Pompeii, about a gladiator named Celadus*

Tabula rasa.
A blank sheet.
> *Latin phrase*

Taedium vitae.
Weariness of life.
> *Latin phrase*

Terminus a quo, terminus ad quem.
Starting point, finishing point.
> *Latin phrase*

Terra incognita.
Unknown territory.
> *Latin phrase*

Tertium quid.
A third possibility or participant.
> *Latin expression, often about negotiations*

Tu quoque.
You too.
> *Latin phrase*

Ultima ratio regum.
The final argument of kings.
   Inscription on Louis XIV's cannon

Usque ad aras.
Even to the altars (i.e. to the last extremity).
   Roman phrase

Uti possidetis.
Keep what you hold.
   Latin phrase, mainly diplomatic

Vade mecum.
Go with me.
   Latin phrase, generally of a companionable book

Vice versa.
Changed around.
   Latin phrase

Videlicet.
You may see (i.e. 'namely' or 'that is to say').
   Latin phrase, abbreviated in English to 'viz'

Vixit.
He has lived.
   Roman announcement of a death

Vox et praeterea nihil.
A voice and nothing more.
   *Latin phrase, adapted from the Greek, about the
   nightingale*

15

St Thomas Aquinas (1225-74)

Ergo necesse est devenire ad aliquod primum movens, quod a nullo movetur; et hoc omnes intelligunt Deum.

Necessarily, therefore, one comes to a prime mover which has not itself been moved; and this everyone understands to be God.

Apelles (4th century AD)

Ne sutor ultra crepidam.

Let the cobbler stick to his last.

> *Rebuke to a shoemaker who, having justly pointed out an error in the painting of a slipper, went on to more general criticism.*

Augustus (63BC - AD14)

Festina lente.

Hasten slowly.

> *A favourite saying of both Augustus and Titus*

Vare, redde legiones!

Varus, give me back my legions!

> *Lamenting that a Roman army under Quintilius Varus had been wiped out by the German chieftain, Arminius*

St Augustine (354-430)

Audi alteram partem.

Hear what the other side has to say.

> *Moral or legal principle*

Da mihi castitatem et continentiam, sed noli modo.

Give me chastity and continence – but not yet!

Dilige et quod vis fac.
Love and do what you will.

*Fecisti nos ad te et inquietum est cor nostrum donec
requiescat in te.*
Thou has made us for thyself and our heart is restless
until it rests in thee.

Misericordia Domini inter pontem et fontem.
God's mercy may be found between the bridge and
the water. *(c.f. 'Betwixt the stirrup and the ground mercy I
asked, mercy I found'.)*

*Nondum amabam et amare amabam... quaerebam quid
amarem, amans amare.*
I did not yet love, but I was in love with love... I
sought what I might love, loving to love.

*Quid est ergo tempus? Si nemo ex me quaerat, scio; si
quarenti explicare velim, nescio.*
What then is time? If no one asks me, I know; if I
want to explain it to someone who asks me, I don't
know.

Roma locuta est, causa finita est.
Rome has spoken, the matter is settled.

Salus extra ecclesiam non est.
There is no salvation outside the Church.

*Securus iudicat orbis terrarum bonos non esse qui se
dividunt ab orbe terrarum in quacunque parte terrarum.*
It is the calm judgement of the world that those men
cannot be good who in any part of the world cut
themselves off from the world.

*Sero te amavi, pulchritudo tam antiqua et tam nova, sero
te amavi! et ecce intus eras et ego foris et ibi te quaerebam.*
Late have I loved thee, beauty so ancient and so new,
late have I loved thee! And, lo, thou wert within me,
and I was without and sought thee there.

Timeo hominem unius libri.
I fear a man who knows only one book.
Tolle lege, tolle lege.
Take them and read them, take them and read them
(*i.e.* the Sacred Scriptures – he opened them at
Rom.13,13).

> *On hearing a voice from outside, in the manner of a child's
> game*

Aulus Gellius (c 123- c 165)

*Alius quidam veterum poetarum cuius nomen mihi nunc
memoriae non est, veritatem temporis filiam esse dixit.*
Another old poet, whose name I forget, said that truth
is the daughter of time.

Religientem esse oportet, religiosum nefas.
One should be religious but not too religious.

> *Quoting an old poem*

Francis Bacon (1561-1626)
Audacter calumniare, semper aliquid haeret.
Spread libel boldly. Some of it always sticks.

Ipsa scientia potestas est.
Knowledge is power.

Brutus (85-42BC)
Sic semper tyrannis.
May this always be the fate of tyrants.
>   *Attributed to Brutus as he killed Caesar, and exclaimed by*
>   *John Wilkes Booth at the assassination of Lincoln*

Caligula (AD12-41)
Oderint dum metuant.
Let them hate me, provided they fear me.
>   *Also said by Suetonius and Cicero*

Utinam populus Romanus unam cervicem haberet.
Would that the Roman people had only one neck.

Cardinal Caraffa (16th century)
Populus vult decipi. Decipiatur.
The people wish to be deceived. Let them be
deceived.
>   *Attributed to Cardinal Caraffa but probably older*

Cato the Elder (234-149BC)
Delenda est Carthago.
Carthage must be destroyed.
>   *Adding at the end of every speech 'Ceterum censeo*
>   *Carthaginem delendam esse'*

Catullus (84-54BC)

Chommoda dicebat si quando commoda vellet
Dicere et insidias Arrius hinsidias.
Arrius, if he wanted to say 'amenities' would say
hamenities, and instead of 'ambushes' hambushes.

In perpetuum, frater, ave atque vale.
Brother, hail and farewell forever.

Lugete, O Veneres Cupidinesque,
Et quantum est hominum venustiorum.
Passer mortuus est meae puellae,
Passer, deliciae meae puellae.
Mourn, O Loves and Cupids and all people of heart.
Dead is my lady's sparrow, the sparrow that was my
lady's joy.

Nobis cum semel occidit brevis lux, Nox est perpetua una
dormienda.
When our brief day is done, we must sleep through a
single endless night.

Odi et amo. Quare id faciam fortasse requiris.
Nescio: sed fieri sentio, et excrucior.
I hate and I love. Why, you may ask, do I behave in
this way? I don't know; I just know that this is how I
feel, and I am in torment.

Paene insularum, Sirmio, insularumque Ocelle.
Sirmio, bright eye of islands and of almost islands.

Vivamus, mea Lesbia, atque amemus,
Rumoresque senum severiorum
Omnes unius aestimemus assis.
Let us live, my Lesbia, and let us love, and let us value
all the mutterings of grumpy old men at just a
farthing.

Cicero (106-43BC)

Abiit, excessit, evasit, erupit.
He has gone, run off, slipped away, flown the coop.
   About Catiline's flight

Agri non omnes frugiferi sunt.
Not all fields are fruitful.

Amicus Plato, amicus Socrates, sed magis amica veritas.
Plato and Socrates are my friends, but truth is a greater
friend.

Cato mirari se aiebat quod non rideret haruspex haruspicem
cum videret.
Cato used to say that he was amazed one soothsayer
could keep a straight face when he met another.

Cedant arma togae.
Let weapons yield to the gown. (*i.e.* Let us have
discussion instead of war.)

Civis Romanus sum.
I am a Roman citizen.

Cui bono?
To whose advantage?
> *Principle of legal enquiry, quoted by Cicero*

Cum dignitate otium
Leisure with honour

Dum lego, assentior.
While I'm reading I agree.
> *On reading Plato's argument for the immortality of the soul*

Esse oportet ut vivas, non vivere ut edas.
You should eat in order to live, not live in order to eat.

Iuravi lingua, mentem iniuratam gero.
With my tongue I have sworn, but my mind is
unsworn.
> *From Euripides*

*Iustitiae tanta vis est ut ne illi quidem qui maleficio et
scelere pascuntur possint sine ulla particula iustitiae vivere.*
So powerful is the idea of justice that not even those
who thrive on crime and wrongdoing can live without
some touch of it.

Malo cum Platone errare quam cum istis vera sentire.
I would rather be wrong with Plato than right with
those people.

Maximum remedium irae mora est.
Time is the best cure for anger.

Nescire quod antea quam natus sis acciderit, id est semper esse puerum; quid enim est aetas hominis nisi memoria rerum nostrarum cum superiorum aetate contexerit?
To be ignorant of what occurred before one's birth is to be always a child, for what is adult life unless memory enables us to compare the events of our own time with those of earlier periods?

Numquam se minus otiosum esse quam cum otiosus, nec minus solum quam cum solus esset.
(Scipio used to say of himself) Never less idle than when he was at leisure, never less lonely than when alone.

O fortunatam natam, me consule, Romam!
O fortunate Rome, born when I was consul!

O tempora! O mores! Senatus haec intellegit, consul videt; hic tamen vivit.
Oh, what times! What manners! The Senate is aware of these things, the consul sees them; and yet this man is still alive.

> *Cicero's attempt at poetry*

Oderint dum metuant.
Let them hate me, provided they fear me.

> *Also said by Suetonius and, frequently, by Caligula*

Silent leges inter arma.
The laws fall silent when swords are drawn.

Stomachor omnia.
I get cross about everything.
> *On growing old*

Summum bonum.
The ultimate good.
> *Also a philosophers' phrase*

Summum ius summa iniuria.
More law, less justice.

Sir Edward Coke (1552-1634)

Cuius est solum, eius est usque ad caelum et ad inferos.
Whoever owns the land owns everything above it,
even to the sky.
> *Legal maxim*

Pirata est hostis humani generis.
A pirate is the enemy of all mankind.

Tantum bona valent quantum vendi possunt.
Things are worth precisely what they can be sold for.
> *Quoting Justinian*

Council of Trent (1564)

Anathema sit.
May it be accursed.
> *Condemning heresy*

Sir George Croke (1560-1642)

De minimis non curat lex.
The law doesn't concern itself with trifles.

Jacapone da Todi (c 1230-1306)
Stabat Mater dolorosa.
There stood the Mother [the Virgin Mary] in her sorrow.

Fray Luis de Léon (c 1527-91)
Dicebamus hesterno die...
We were saying yesterday...
   On resuming his lectures after five years in prison

Melchior de Polignac (1661-1742)
Errare humanum est.
To err is human.

René Descartes (1596-1650)
Cogito, ergo sum.
I think, therefore I am.

Natura abhorrat vacuum.
Nature abhores a vacuum.

Diogenes (c 400- c 325BC)
In eburna vagina plumbeus gladius.
A leaden sword in an ivory sheath.
   Deriding a showy shallow man

Drunken Barnaby's Journal (1723)
Veni Gotham, ubi multos
Si non omnes vidi stultos.
I came to Gotham, where most of those I saw, if not all, were stupid.
   'The Wise Men of Gotham' being proverbial in the Middle Ages for their stupidity

William Dunbar (c 1465 - c 1513)
Timor mortis conturbat me.
The fear of death troubles me.

Sir James Dyer (1510-82)
Fiat iustitia, ruat coelum.
Let justice be done though the heavens fall.
   Legal maxim

Ennius (239-169BC)
At tuba terribili sonitu taratantara dixit.
And the trumpet in terrible tones went taratantara.

O Tite tute Tati tibi tanta tyranne tulisti!
O tyrant Titus Tatius, what a lot you brought upon
yourself!

*Unus homo nobis cunctando restituit rem; Non ponebat
enim rumores ante salutem.*
By delay one man saved everything for us; he cared more
about the safety of the state than about public opinion.
   *About Fabius Cunctator, who, for a long while, avoided
   battle with Hannibal*

Flavius Vegetius Renatus (early 5th century)
Qui desiderat pacem praeparet bellum.
Whoever desires peace should prepare for war.

Gaius (c 1st century AD)
Damnosa hereditas.
A ruinous inheritance.
   Inst; legal term

Pope Gregory the Great (c 540-604)
Non Angli sed angeli.
Not Angles but angels.
> *On seeing some handsome English boys in the marketplace*

Emperor Hadrian (76-138)
Animula, vagula, blandula,
Hospes comesque corporis,
Quae nunc abibis in loca,
Pallidula, frigida, nudula,
Nec, ut soles, dabis iocos?
> *Little soul of mine, frolicsome, pleasant, guest and comrade*
> *of my body, where are you going, pale, cold, unprotected,*
> *never again to jest, as you are accustomed to do?*
> *On dying, to his soul*

Hippocrates (c 460 - c 357BC)
Ars longa, vita brevis.
Life is short, the art so long to learn
> *Roman translation of Hippocrates' aphorism*

Horace (65-8BC)
Aequam memento rebus in arduis
Servare mentem.
In difficult times, keep calm.

Aes triplex.
Triple bronze (*i.e.* immensely durable).

Age iam meorum
Finis amorum.
Come then, last of my loves.

Amphora coepit
Institui; currente rota cur urceus exit?
It was intended to be a vase. Why does it emerge from
the potter's wheel a mere jug?

Atque sciebat quae sibi barbarus tortor pararet.
Well he knw what was being prepared for him by the
savage tormentor.

Auream quisquis mediocritatem Diligit.
Whoever loves the golden mean.

Beatus ille, qui procul negotiis,
Ut prisca gens mortalium,
Paterna rura bobus exercet suis,
Solutus omni faenore.
Happy is he who, far away from business, ploughs
ancestral acres, free from financial worries, like the
earliest race of men.

Brevis esse laboro,
Obscurus fio.
I strive to be brief, I become obscure.

Caelo tonantem credimus Iovem regnare.
When he thunders in the sky we believe that Jupiter
reigns.

Caelum non animum mutant qui trans mare currunt.
They change their skies but not their minds who rush
across the sea.

Cras ingens iterabimus aequor.
Tomorrow we shall set out once more upon the vast
sea.

Credite posteri.
Believe it, posterity.

Diffugee nives, redeunt iam gramina campis arboribusque
comae.
The snows have fled, grass returns to the fields and
leaf to the trees.

Dulce et decorum est pro patria mori.
It is sweet and seemly to die for one's country.

Dulce ridentem Lalagen amabo,
Dulce loquentem.
I will love Lalage, sweetly smiling, sweetly talking.

Durum! Sed levius fit patientia
Quicquid corrigere est nefas.
It's hard! But what cannot be mended becomes lighter
with patience.

Eheu! Fugaces, Postume, Postume,
Labuntur anni; nec pietasmoram
Rugis et instanti senectae
Afferet indomitaeque morti.
Alas, Postumus, the fleeting years slip by, nor can piety
delay the coming of wrinkles or approaching old age or
unconquerable death.

Epicuri de grege porcum.
A pig from Epicurus's herd.
   About himself

Et hoc genus omne.
And everything [or everyone] of that kind.

Exegi monumentum aere perennius.
I have built a monument more enduring than brass.
   Of his poetry

Favete linguis.
Speak propitiously (or maintain a holy silence).
   A phrase which introduced sacred ceremonies

Gradus ad Parnassum.
The path to Parnassus.
traditional name for a Latin verse textbook
Heu quotiens fidem
Mutatosque deos flebit et aspera
Nigris aequora ventis
Emirabitur insolens,
Qui nunc te fruitur credulus aurea,
Qui semper vacuam, semper amabilem
Sperat, nescius aurae
Fallacis.
Alas, how often shall he weep for faith and gods so
changed, and, from lack of experience, marvel at the
waters rough beneath the darkening gales, who now
enjoys you, naïvely thinking you pure gold, hoping
that you will always be free of heart, always lovable –
little he knows of the treacherous wind.

Hinc illae lacrimae.
Hence (*i.e.* consequently) those tears.
   Also said by Terence

Ille terrarum mihi praeter omnes
Angulus ridet.
That little corner of the world charms me beyond all
others.

Illi robur et aes triplex
Circa pectus erat, qui fragilem truci Commisit pelago ratem
Primus.
He must have had a heart of oak encircled with
threefold bronze who first launched a frail bark upon
the raging sea.

Indignor quandoque bonus dormitat Homerus.
I am censorious when great Homer nods.

Integer vitae scelerisque purus non eget Mauris iaculis
neque arcu nec venenatis gravida sagittis, Fusce, pharetra.
A man of upright life, unstained by guilt, needs no
Moorish javelins, Fuscus, nor bow nor quiver laden
with poisoned arrows.

Intermissa, Venus, diu rursus bella moves. Parce, precor,
precor.
After a long interval of peace, you attack me again,
Venus. Spare me, I pray you, I pray you.

Inter silvas Academi quaerere verum.
To seek the truth amid the groves of Academus.

Isne tibi melius suadet, qui 'rem facias, rem, si possis,
recte, si non, quocumque modo, rem'?
Does he advise you better who tells you, 'Wealth,
acquire wealth; honestly if you can; if not, by any
means available'?

Itermissa, Venus, diu rursus bella moves. Parce, precor,
precor.
After a long interval of peace, you attack me again,
Venus. Spare me, I pray you, I pray you.

Iustum et tenacem propositi virum
Non civium ardor prava iubentium,
Non voltus instantis tyranni,
Mente quatit solida.
The just man, firm of purpose, is not moved from his
resolution either by his fellow citizens urging iniquity
or by the tyrant's threatening countenance.

Laudator temporis acti.
A praiser of past times.

Magnas inter opes inops.
Poverty amidst great wealth.
> *Palmerston's reply to Kentish hop-growers who complained*
> *that their crop had suffered more from bad weather than*
> *crops in surrounding districts*

Mentis gratissimus error.
A most delightful wandering of the mind.

Militavi non sine gloria.
I have fought not without glory.
> *About the battles of love*

Misce stultitiam consiliis brevem:
Dulce est desipere in loco.
Blend a little foolishness with your wisdom: it's nice
to be silly at the right moment.

Miseri, quibus intentata nites.
Unhappy are they for whom you shine untested.
> *About a fickle girl*

Mobilium turba Quiritium.
A crowd of inconstant citizens.
> *Origin of the phrase 'the mob'*

Mutato nomine de te
Fabula narratur.
Change the name, and the story is about you.

Natis in usum laetitiae scyphis
Pugnare Thracum est; tollite barbarum Morem.
Fighting over one's cups, which were made for
pleasure, is a Thracian habit; away with such
barbarous doings.

Narratur et prisci Catonis
Saepe mero caluisse virtus.
They say that even old Cato's stern disposition was
often warmed by wine.

Naturam expelles furca, tamen usque recurret.
You may drive nature out with a pitchfork but she will always return.

Nec gemino bellum Troianum orditur ab ovo.
Nor does he start the Trojan war from the twin eggs (*i.e.* from Helen's birth).

Neque semper arcum.
Tendit Apollo.
Nor is Apollo always bending his bow.

Nescio quid curtae semper abest rei.
No state of affairs is ever perfect.

Nescit vox missa reverti.
A word once uttered cannot be recalled.

Nihil est ab omni Parte beatum.
Nothing is entirely good.

Nil desperandum Teucro duce et auspice Teucro.
We must not despair while Teucer is our leader and we are under Teucer's banner.

Nocturna versate manu, versate diurna.
Turn these things over by night, turn them over all day long.

Non cuivis homini contingit adire Corinthum.
It's not given to everybody to visit Corinth (a luxurious holiday spot).

Non ego hoc ferrem, calidus iuventa, Consule Planco.
I wouldn't have put up with such treatment in my
hot-blooded youth when Plancus was consul.

Non ego ventosae venor suffragia plebis.
I don't pursue the votes of the fickle masses.

Non omnis moriar; multaque pars mei Vitabit Libitinam.
I shall not wholly die; a great part of me will escape
Libitina [the goddess of funerals].

Non sum qualis eram bonae sub regno Cynarae.
I'm not the man I used to be when sweet Cynara
ruled my heart.

Non tamen intus
Digna geri promes in scenam.
You should not put upon the stage things which
would occur more suitably behind the scenes.

Nonumque prematur in annum.
Let it be kept back for nine years.
   Of a literary work

Nullius addictus iurare in verba magistri.
Not bound to swear by the words of any master.

Nunc est bibendum, nunc pede libero
Pulsanda tellus.
Now is the time for drinking, now let the ground
shake beneath a lively dance.

O fons Bandusiae, splendidior vitro.
O spring of Bandusia, brighter than glass.

O matre pulchra filia pulchrior.
Oh daughter, more beautiful than your beautiful mother.

O noctes cenaeque deum.
O nights and feasts of the gods.

Odi profanum vulgus et arceo.
I hate and spurn the common crowd.

Pallida mors aequo pulsat pede pauperum tabernas
Regumque turres. O beate Sesti,
Vitae summa brevis spem nos vetat incohare longam.
Pale death knocks with impartial foot on the hovels of
the poor and the palaces of kings. Oh happy Sestus,
life's brief sum forbids us to form any long-term hope.

Parcus deorum cultor et infrequens
Insanientis dum sapientiae
Consultus erro; nunc retrorsum
Vela dare atque iterare cursus
Cogor relictos.
A grudging and infrequent worshipper of the gods
while I wandered professing a wisdom which was no
wisdom, I am forced now to re-set my sails and follow
again the course I had abandoned.

Parturiunt montes, nascetur ridiculus mus.
The mountains are in labour, and a silly mouse will be
born.

Persicos odi, puer, apparatus.
I hate, my boy, those Persian fripperies.

Populus me sibilat: at mihi plaudo.
The people hiss me: but I applaud myself.

Post equitem sedet atra cura.
Black care sits behind the rider.

Pulvis et umbra sumus.
We are dust and shadow.

Purpureus late qui splendeat unus et alter
Assuitur pannus.
One or two brightly shining purple patches are sewn
on.

Quan si clientum longa negotia diiudicata lite relingueret,
tendens Venafranos in agros, aut Lacedaemonium
Tarentum.
As though, with his client's weary business finally
resolved, he were setting out for this Venafran fiends
or Doria Tarentum.

Quamquam ridentem dicere verum
Quid vetat?
Nevertheless, what prevents us from telling the truth
cheerfully?

Quem si puellarum insereres choro,
Mire sagaces falleret hospites
Discrimen obscurum, solutis

Crinibus ambiguoque vultu.
If you were to place him in a throng of girls, the most
discerning strangers could hardly tell the difference,
with his flowing locks and his androgynous face.

Quis desiderio sit pudor aut modus
Tam cari capitis?
What shame should there be or limit in our longing
for one so dear?

Relicta non bene parmula.
My little shield ingloriously discarded.
    Confessing that he ran away from the battle at Philippi

Semel emissum volat irrevocabile verbum.
A word once spoken flies beyond recall.

Semper ad eventum festinat et in medias res non secus ad
notas auditorem rapit.
He always hurries to the outcome and plunges his
listener into the middle of things as though they were
already familiar with them.

Sesquipedelia verba.
Words a foot and a half long.

Si fractus inlabatur orbis, impavidum ferient ruinae.
If the world were to break and fall upon him, he
would be unafraid as the wreckage struck.

Si volet usus,
Quem penes arbitrium est et ius et norma loquendi.
If usage sanctions it – this is the criterion, the law and
the practice of language.

Sic me servavit Apollo.
Thus Apollo saved me.
> *On being rescued from the attentions of a garrulous fellow*

Simplex munditiis.
Simple in her neatness.

Spatio brevi
Spem longam reseces. Dum loquimur fugerit invida
Aetas. Carpe diem, quam minimum credula postero.
Confine your hopes to a short space. While we talk,
envious time has been flying. Seize today, trust as little as
possible to the morrow.

Splendide mendax.
Gloriously false.

Sublimi feriam sidera vertice.
In exaltation I shall smite the stars.

Tecum vivere amem, tecum obeam libens.
With thee I would love to live, with thee I would
gladly die.

Tempus edax rerum.
Time that devours all things.

Teres atque rotundus.
A man smooth and plump.

Velut inter ignes
Luna minores.
Like the moon among the lesser lights.

Vestigia terrent
Omnia in adversum spectantia, nulla retorsum.
The tracks frighten me, all going towards you but none
returning.
   Said by the wily fox to the lion at the entrance to his den

Vides ut alta stet nive candidum
Soracte, nec iam sustineant onus
Silvae laborantes.
You see how Soracte stands white in deep snow and
the burdened woods can no longer bear the weight.

Vixere fortes ante Agamemnona
Multi; sed omnes illacrimabiles
Urgentur ignotique longa
Nocte, carent quia vate sacro.
Many brave men lived before Agamemnon but,
unlamented and unknown, they are all swallowed up
in long darkness, because they found no holy poet.

John Huss (c 1372-1415)
O sancta simplicitas!
What holy simplicity!
   When, as he was burnt at the stake, he saw an old peasant
   bringing extra faggots

St Jerome (342-420)

Pereant illi qui ante nos nostra dixerunt.
May they perish who have made our own good remarks
before us.

> *Quoting Aelius Donatus*

Samuel Johnson (1709-84)

Nullum quod tetigit non ornavit.
He touched nothing which he did not adorn.

> *Epitaph on Oliver Goldsmith*

Julian the Apostate (c 332-363)

Vicisti Galilaee.
Thou has conquered, O Galilean.

Julius Caesar (100-44BC)

Aut Caesar aut nullus.
I will be Caesar or nothing.
Imperial motto for the ambitious

Et tu, Brute!
Even you, Brutus!

> *Latin version of Caesar's cry at his assassination, uttered in Greek*

Gallia est omnis divisa in partes tres.
The whole of Gaul is divided into three parts.

Iacta alea est.
The die is cast.

> *A Roman expression, but used most famously by Caesar when he crossed the Rubicon*

Meos tam suspicione quam crimine iudico carere oportere.
I consider that my own family should be not only
guiltless but above suspicion.

Veni, vidi, vici.
I came, I saw, I conquered.
> *Reporting to the Senate his victory over Pharnaces*

Justinian (483-565)

Actus non facit reum nisi mens sit rea.
A guilty intention, not just the act, makes a man
guilty.
> *Institutes*

*Justitia est constans et perpetua voluntas just suum cuique
tribuendi.*
Justice is the constant and perpetual urge to award to
each his due.
> *Ibid.*

Juvenal (60-130)

Cantabit vacuus coram latrone viator.
The penniless traveller will sing in the presence of a
robber.

Galeatum sero duelli paenitet.
Once you've got your helmet on it's too late to regret
the battle.

Mens sana in corpore sano.
A healthy mind in a healthy body.

Nequeo monstrare, et sentio tantum.
I can't demonstrate it; I just feel it.

Nulla fere causa est in qua non femina litem moverit.
There are hardly any legal disputes which weren't
started by a woman.

O si sic omnia! or *O si sic omnes!*
Oh that all things [or all men] were like this!

Occidit miseros crambe repetita magistros.
Re-cooked cabbage is the death of these unhappy
teachers.
> *About schoolmasters*

Panem et circenses.
Bread and circuses.
> *Saying that this was all the decadent Roman people cared
> about*

Pone seram, cohibe; sed quis custodiet ipsos Custodes?
Shoot the bolt, close the door; but who is to guard the
guardians?

Servata semper lege et ratione loquendi.
Always keep to the rules and logic of language.

Si natura negat, facit indignatio versum.
If talent fails, anger prompts a verse.

Tenet insanabile multos scribendi cacoethes.
An incurable itch for writing seizes many people.

Laberius (107-43BC)
Amare et sapere vix deo conceditur.
To love and be wise is hardly granted even to a god.

The Law
Aestimes iudicia, non numeres.
You should weigh opinions, not count them.

Caveat emptor.
Let the buyer beware.

Dum se bene gesserit.
So long as he conducts himself properly.
   Expression, specifying the tenure of judges

Habeas corpus.
You are to present the body
   e.g. when a person is, allegedly, being wrongly held in prison

In flagranti delicto.
In the very act of crime.

In forma pauperis.
As a pauper (and therefore entitled to free legal aid).

Iudicium parium aut leges terrae.
The judgement of his peers or the laws of the land.
   (Only by these may an Englishman be convicted.)
   Magna Carta

44

Lex talionis.
The law of retaliation.

Locum tenens.
Occupying his place.
> *A deputy (e.g. a doctor standing in for another)*

Locus paenitentiae
An opportunity to change one's mind.

Locus standi.
A standing place
> *i.e. the right to be in court or on a committee*

Malum in se. Malum prohibitum.
Something inherently wrong as distinct from
something wrong because there is a law against it.

Mandamus.
We order.
> *A writ ordering someone to do something*

Mansuetae naturae.
Of a gentle disposition
> *Legal phrase generally of domestic as opposed to wild
> animals ('ferae naturae')*

Nolle prosequi.
Unwillingness to prosecute.

Nulli negabimus, nulli deferemus iustitiam.
To no man will we deny, to no man will we delay,
justice.
  Magna Carta

Quantum meruit.
As much as it was worth.
  Phrase quantifying money due for a service

Res ipsa loquitur.
The thing speaks for itself.

Res iudicata.
A matter which has been settled.

Res nullius.
A thing which belongs to no-one.

Sine die.
Without a fixed day (*i.e.* for reassembly; indefinitely).

Sub judice.
Currently the subject of legal action.

Uberrima fides.
Fullest good faith
  (*e.g. as a term of contract*)

Volenti non fit injuria.
No wrong is done to one who submitted to it
willingly.

Livy (59BC - AD17)
Intoleranda Romanis vox, Vae victis!
'Woe to the conquered!', a saying intolerable to
Romans.
    Recalling Brennus the Gaul's insult

Emperor Lothar I (attrib., 9th century)
Tempora mutantur, nos et mutamur in illis.
Times change and we change with them.

Lucan (39-65)
Magni nominis umbra.
The shadow of a great name.

Victrix causa deis placuit sed victa Catoni.
The gods favoured the triumphant cause, Cato the lost
cause.

Nil actum credens dum quid superesset agendum.
Considering nothing done while anything remained to
be done.
    Of Julius Caesar

Lucretius (94-55BC)
Ex nihilo nihil fit.
Nothing comes of nothing.

*Medio de fonte leporum Surgit amari aliquid quod in ipsis
floribus angat.*
From amidst the fountain of delight something bitter
springs to trouble us even among the flowers.

Suave mari magno turbantibus aequora ventis
E terra magnum alterius spectare laborem.
It is agreeable, when out at sea the winds are
whipping up the waves, to watch from shore another's
trouble.

Martin Luther (1485-1546)
Esto peccator et pecca fortiter, sed fortius fide et gaude in
Christo.
Be a sinner and sin strongly, but more strongly have
faith and rejoice in Christ.

Walter Mapes (c 1140-1210)
Meum est propositum in taberna mori.
I mean to die in a pub.

> *A mediaeval drinking song*

Martial (c 40 - c 104)
Non amo te, Sabidi, nec possum dicere quare;
Hoc tantum possum dicere, non amo te.
I don't like you, Sabidius, but I can't say why; all I can
say is that I don't like you.

> *Famously applied by Tom Brown, when an undergraduate,*
> *to the Dean of Christ Church: I do not love thee, Doctor*
> *Fell,/The reason why I cannot tell;/But this I know, and*
> *know full well,/I do not love thee, Doctor Fell.*

Non scribit, cuius carmina nemo legit.
A man whose work nobody reads isn't a writer.

Rus in urbe.
A bit of country in the town.

Nero (37-68)

Qualis artifex pereo.
What an artist dies in me.
   Just before his death

William of Occam (1285-1349)

Entia non sunt multiplicanda praeter necessitatem.
Entities [*i.e.*philosophic or economic concepts] should
not be multiplied unnecessarily.
   Occam's 'razor'

Frustra fit per plura quod potest fieri per pauciora.
It is wasteful to use more things for what can be done
with fewer.

Ovid (43BC - c AD17)

Abeunt studia in mores.
Things practised become second nature.

Candida me capiet, capiet me flava puella.
I shall fall for the ash-blonde – and the tawny haired
girl too.

Emax domina.
The lady is addicted to shopping.

Expedit esse deos, et, ut expedit esse, putemus.
It is expedient that there should be gods, and, since it
is expedient, let us assume that there are.

In medio tutissimus ibis.
The middle is the safest course.

Iuppiter ex alto periuria ridet amantum.
Jupiter smiles from on high at lovers' lies.

Omina sunt aliquid.
There is something in omens.

Rara avis in terries, nigroque simillima cygno.
A bird rarely seen on earth, very like a black swan.
> But 'rara avis' occurs also in Horace and Juvenal

Spectatum veniunt, veniunt spectentur ut ipsae.
The women come to see the show, and they come
to be seen.

Video meliora proboque;
Deteriora sequor
I see and approve what is better, but I follow the worse.

Count Oxenstierna (1583-1654)
Nescis, mi fili, quantula sapientia gubernetur mundus?
Do you not know, my son, with how little wisdom the
world is governed?
> Writing to his son

Persius (34-62)
At pulchrum est digito monstrari et dicier, Hic est.
It's a sweet thing to be pointed out and have it said,
'That's him.'

De nihilo nihil, in nihilum nil posse reverti.
Nothing come from nothing, and nothing which exists
can become nothing.

Pervigilium Veneris (? 2nd century AD)
Cras amet qui nunquam amavit quique amavit cras amet.
Tomorrow he shall love who has never loved before,
and he who has loved shall love tomorrow.

Petronius Arbiter (died AD65)
Cave canem.
Beware of the dog.
> *Describing a notice beside the door*

Curiosa felicitas.
Studied felicity (of style).
> *Referring to Horace*

Phaedrus (1st century AD)
Gratis anhelans, multa agendo nihil agens.
Puffing pointlessly, very busy doing nothing.

O quanta species cerebrum non habet!
O that such beauty should be brainless!

Plautus (c 25-184BC)
Anguilla est, elabitur.
He's an eel; he slips away.

Dictum sapienti sat est.
A word to the wise is enough.
also said by Terence

Quem di diligunt adolescens moritur.
Whom the gods love dies young.

Rem acu tetigisti.
You've touched the thing with a needle (*i.e.* hit the spot).
> *Quoted by Jeeves in PG Wodehouse*

Ubi mel ibi apes.
Where there is honey there will be bees.

Pliny the Elder (23-79)
Addito salis grano.
With a grain of salt.
> *More commonly 'Cum grano salis'*

Pliny the Younger (born c 61)
Ex Africa semper aliquid novi.
There's always something new from Africa.
> *Slightly misquoted; actually 'Vulgare Graeciae dictum,*
> *Semper Africam aliquid novi afferre.' The common Greek*
> *saying that there is always something new out of Africa*

Nihil aeque gratum est adeptis quam concupescentibus.
Nothing is as pleasing when one has obtained it as
when one desired it.

Vita hominum altos recessus magnasque latebras habet.
A man's life contains hidden depths and large secret
areas.

Pontius Pilate (1st century AD)
Ecce homo!
Behold the man!
> *John XIX.5; often used as title for pictures of Jesus wearing*
> *the crown of thorns*

Propertius (c 50 - later than 16BC)
In magnis et voluisse sat est.
In great endeavours the intention is enough.

Proverbs
Ab ovo usque ad mala.
From egg to apples.
> *Referring to the courses of a Roman dinner, or 'from soup to nuts'*

Finis coronat opus.
The end crowns the work.

In vino veritas.
Under the influence of wine, the truth emerges.

Interdum stultus bene loquitur.
Occasionally a fool says something sensible.

Laborare est orare.
To work is to pray.

Latrante uno, latrat statim et alter canis.
When one dog barks another immediately barks too.

Malum vas non frangitur.
A worthless vase doesn't get broken.

Nisi caste, saltem caute.
If not chastely, at least cautiously.

Olet lucernam.
It smells of the lamp.
   About some literary work

Omne animal post coitum triste.
After making love all creatures are sad.

Ovis ovem sequitur.
One sheep follows another.

Pons asinorum.
The asses' bridge.
   Proverbially the Fifth Proposition of Euclid

Post bellum auxilium.
Help – after the war.

Prospectandum vetulo latrante.
When an old dog barks, look out.

Quem deus vult perdere prius dementat.
Whom God wishes to destroy he first makes mad.
   Adapted from Publilius Syrus

Qui me amat, amat et canem meum.
Who loves me loves my dog too.
   Quoted by St Bernard

Quieta non moveri.
Leave well alone.

Quod licet Iovi non licet bovi.
What is permissable for Jove is not permissible for an ox.

Ululas Athenas portas.
You are taking owls to Athens (*i.e.* coals to Newcastle).

Verbum sapienti sat est.
A word is enough for the wise.

Publilius Syrus (1st century BC)
Fortuna vitrea est: tum cum splendet frangitur.
Fortune is like glass: as it shines, it shatters.

Misere est tacere cogi quod copias loqui.
It's wretched being forced to keep quiet about something one's bursting to tell.

Quintilian (c 35 - c 96)
Dum deliberamus quando incipiendum est, incipere iam serum est.
While we debate when a start should be made, it is already too late to start.

Lucus a non lucendo.
Lit: A grove because there is no light there; 'lucus', a grove, being supposedly derived from 'lucere', to shine.
  Ridiculing etymological guesswork

Inanis verborum torrens.
A meaningless torrent of words.

Non ut edam vivo, sedut vivam edo.
I do not live to eat, but eat to live.

Rabelais (c 1494 - c 1553)
Chimaera bombinans in vacuo.
An imaginary monster buzzing in empty space.

Religion
Agnus Dei, misereri nobis.
Lamb of God, have pity on us.
   The Roman Catholic Missal

Annuncio vobis gaudium magnum. Habemus Papam.
I bring you tidings of great joy. We have a Pope.
   *The announcement from the Vatican that a new Pope has
   been elected*

Cantate Domino.
Sing unto the Lord.
   The Vulgate, 97th Psalm (BCP 98th)

Deo optimo maximo.
To God, the sum of all goodness, the sum of all
greatness.
   Roman Catholic slogan, usually just DOM

*De profundis clamavi ad te,
Domine; Domine, exaudi vocem meam.*
Up from the depths I have cried to thee, Lord; Lord,
hear my voice.
   The Vulgate, 129th Psalm (BCP 130th)

Deo volente.
God willing.
>   *Latin expression, often just DV*

Deus ex machina.
A god from the machine. Referring (lit.) to the god
who, in some classical plays, descends, with special
effects, to solve the problem.

Dominus vobiscum.
The Lord be with you.
>   *The Roman Catholic Missal*

Ecce homo!
Behold the man.
>   *Pontius Pilate; John XIX.5; often used as title for pictures of
>   Jesus wearing the crown of thorns*

Fiat lux.
Let there be light
>   *The Vulgate, Genesis 1.3*

Fidei Defensor.
Defender of the Faith.
>   *Ecclesiastical title used mainly by British Sovereigns since
>   Henry VIII was given it by the Pope*

Imprimatur.
It may be printed.
>   *A censor's permission, especially in the Catholic Church*

In partibus infidelium.
In the lands of the infidel.
> *Ecclesiastical expression, as of a bishop without a see in*
> *Christendom*

In pectore.
Hidden in his breast.
> *Roman Catholic ecclesiastical term, referring to cardinals*
> *whose names the Pope does not publish*

In te, Domine, speravi: non confundar in aeternum.
In thee, Lord, have I placed my hope: let me never be
confounded.
> *The Vulgate, 70th Psalm (BCP 71st), and the last verse of*
> *the Te Deum*

Ite, missa est.
Go, the Mass is ended.
> *The Roman Catholic Missal*

INRI (Iesus Nazarenus Rex Iudaeorum).
Jesus of Nazareth, King of the Jews.
> *The inscription above the cross*

Magna est veritas et praevalet.
The truth is great and it prevails.
> *The Vulgate, III Edras 4.41*

Mea culpa, mea maxima culpa.
My fault, my very great fault.
> *Christian liturgical phrase*

Noli me tangere.
Touch me not.
> *The Vulgate, John 20.17*

Nolo episcopari.
I don't want to be made a bishop.
> *Ecclesiastical expression, implying a suitable modesty*

Non nobis, Domine.
Not unto us, O Lord (...but unto thy name give glory).
> *The Vulgate, 113th Psalm, 2nd part (BCP 115th)*

Nunc dimittis.
Now lettest thou [thy servant] depart.
> *The Vulgate, Luke 2.29*

O Sancte Pater, sic transit gloria mundi.
Holy Father, thus passes away the glory of this world.
> *Reminder to the Popes during their enthronement,*
> *accompanied by the burning of flax*

Pax vobiscum.
Peace be with you.
> *The Roman Catholic Missal*

Quo vadis?
Where are you going?
> *Christ, appearing to St Peter as he fled from Rome*

Requiem aeternam dona eis, Domine.
Give them eternal rest, O Lord.
> *Beginning of the Roman Catholic Mass for the Dead*

Requiescat in pace.
May he rest in peace.
> *Often simply 'RIP' on tombstones*

Stare super antiquas vias, et videre quaeam sit via recta et bona, et ambulare in ea.
To stand upon the old ways, and to see which is the straight and good road, and to walk in it.
> *The Vulgate, Jeremiah, 6.16, quoted in Bacon's essay 'Of Innovations'*

Sursum corda.
Lift up your hearts.
> *The missal*

Tuba mirum spargens sonum.
The trumpet sending forth its marvellous sound.
> *A line from the Dies irae*

Urbi et orbi.
To the city and the world.
> *Papal benediction*

Vade retro, Satana.
Get thee behind me, Satan.
> *The Vulgate, Luke 4.8*

Vanitas vanitatum. Omnia vanitas.
Vanity of vanities. All is vanity.
> *The Vulgate, Ecclesiastes 1.2*

Sarpi, Father Paul (1552-1623)
Esto perpetua.
May you last forever.
> *Dying words about his native Venice*

Seneca (c 4BC - AD65)
Omnis ars imitatio est naturae.
All art is an imitation of nature.

Manus manum lavat.
One hand washes the other.

Nemo fit fato nocens.
No one is driven to crime by fate.

Spinoza (1632-77)
Sub specie aeternitatis.
In the sight of eternity.
> *Theological expression*

Stesichorus (7-6 centuries BC)
Palinodum canere.
To sing a palinode.
> *Recanting in a new poem an earlier one in which he had slighted Helen*

Suetonius (early 2nd century AD)
Cum aliquos numquam soluturos significare vult, 'ad Kalendas Graecas soluturos' ait.
When he [Augustus] wanted to suggest that a debt would never be paid he used to say, 'it will be paid on the Greek calends' (*i.e.* never).

Iure sit gloriatus marmoream se relinquere quam latericiam accepisset.
He could rightly boast that he found a city of brick and left a city of marble.
  About Augustus

Oderint dum metuant.
Let them hate me, provided they fear me.
  Also frequently said by Cicero and Caligula

Tacitus (56 - later than 117)

Arbiter elegantiae.
A judge of elegant manners or objects.
  About Petronius

Corruptissima in republica plurimae leges.
The most corrupt state will have the most laws.

Ego facilius crediderim naturam margaritas deesse quam nobis avaritiam.
Personally, I could more easiliy believe that the pearls lacked quality than that men lacked greed.
  On the low level of pearl fishing in Britain

Imperium Traiani, rara temporum felicitate, ubi sentire quae velis et quae sentias dicere licet.
The reign of Trajan, a rare and happy time when one might think what one pleased and say what one thought.

Inauditi atque indefensi, tamquam innocentes perierant.
They were condemned unheard and undefended, just as though they were innocent.

Intuta quae indecora.
What is unseemly is unsafe.

Memoriae proditur Tiberium, quotiens curia egrederetur,
Graecis verbis in hunc modum eloqui solitum: 'O homines
ad servitutem paratos!'
Tradition says that Tiberius, whenever he left the
Senate House, used to exclaim in Greek, 'How ready
these men are to be slaves!'

Omne ignotum pro magnifico.
The unknown is always taken to be grand.

Omnium consensu capax imperii nisi imperasset.
Universally judged fit to rule – until he ruled.
about the Emperor Galba

Proprium humani ingenii est odisse quem laeseris.
It is human nature to hate someone you have injured.

Rara temporum felicitate, ubi sentire quae veils, et quae
sentias dicere licet.
The rare happiness of times when you may think waht
you like and say what you think.

Solitudinem faciunt, pacem appellant.
They make a desert and call it peace.

Terence (c 190-159)
Amantium irae amoris integratio.
Lovers' quarrels are the renewal of love.

Dictum sapienti sat est.
A word to the wise is enough.
   Also said by Plautus

Fortes fortuna adiuvat.
Fortune favours the brave.

Homo sum; humani nil a me alienum puto.
I am a man; everything human is of concern to me.
   *(St Augustine says that, when these words were spoken in
   the theatre, the audience applauded thunderously)*

Non id videndum, coniugum ut bonis bona
At ut ingenium congruat et mores moribus;
Probitas pudorque virgini dos optima est.
What matters is not that a married couple should be
equal in wealth but that their minds and manners
should be compatible; integrity and modesty are a
girl's best dowry.

Nullum est iam dictum quod non sit dictum prius
Nothing is said today which hasn't been said before.

Obsequium amicos, veritas odium parit.
Obsequiousness begets friends, truth begets hatred.

Quot homines tot sententiae.
As many opinions as there are people.

Sine Cerere et Libero friget venus.
Without food and wine love grows cold.

Vos valete et plaudite.
Farewell – and applaud!
> *Customary invitation to applaud at the end of a Roman comedy*

Terentianus Maurus (late 2nd century)
Habent sua fata libelli.
Books have their own destiny.

Tertullian (c 160 - c 225)
Certum est quia impossibile.
Assuredly true because it seems impossible.
> *On the resurrection*

O testimonium animae naturaliter Christianae!
O evidence of a mind naturally Christian!
> *(i.e. the belief in a supreme being, without benefit of Christian revelation)*

Thomas of Celano (attrib., early 13th century)
Dies irae, dies illa,
Solvet saeclum in favilla
Teste David cum Sybilla
Day of wrath, that day which shall dissolve the world into ashes, as both David and the Sybil testify.

Emperor Titus (39-81)
Amici, diem perdidi.
Friends, I have lost a day.
> *Having done nothing to help anybody all day*

Vespasian (9-79)

Non olet.
It doesn't smell.
> *About a coin charged for the use of public lavatories*

Vae! Puto deus fio.
Alas, I think I am becoming a god.
> *When dying*

St Vincent of Lerins (5th century)

Quod ubique, quod semper, quo dab omnibus creditum est.
What has everywhere, always and by everyone been believed.

Virgil (70-19BC)

Agnosco veteris vestigia flammae.
I recognise the traces of an old flame.

Ambo florentes aetatibus, Arcades ambo,
Et cantare pares et respondere parati.
They were both in the flower of their youth together,
Arcadians both, ready to sing and ready to respond.

Animum pictura pascit imani.
He feeds his mind on an empty picture.

Arma virumque cano.
Arms and the man I sing.
> *First words of the Aeneid*

Decus et tutamen.
Handsome and secure.
   Inscribed on the English £1 coin

Dis aliter visum.
The gods decided otherwise.

Disce, puer, virtutem ex me, verumque laborem,
Fortunam ex aliis.
Learn from me, boy, courage and exertion, good
fortune from others.

Dulcis moriens reminiscitur Argos.
Dying, he remembers his dear Argos.

Dux femina facti.
The leader of this enterprise was a woman.

E pluribus unum.
Several become one.
   Attrib., formerly the motto of the USA

Facilis descensus Averno,
Sed revocare gradus superasque evadere ad auras
Hoc opus, hic labor est.
Easy is the descent to hell, but retracing one's steps
and regaining the open air, that's very hard work

Felix qui potuit rerum cognoscere causas
Atque metus omnes et inexorabile fatum
Subiecit pedibus strepitumque Acherontis avari.
Happy is he who has been able to understand the
cause of things, and to tread beneath his feet all fear
and unyielding fate and the noise of death's greedy
stream.

> *Of Lucretius*

Fidus Achates.
Faithful Achates.

> **Referring to the companion of Aeneas, but used now of any
> close friend**

Forsan et haec olim meminisse iuvabit.
Perhaps one day even these things will be a pleasure
to recall.

Fuit Ilium.
Troy was (*i.e.* and is no more).

Genus immortale manet, multosque per annos
Stat fortuna domus, et avi numerantur avorum.
The race dies not; through many years the fortunes of
the house stand firm, and its children's children
multiply.

Hae tibi erunt artes, pacique imponere morem,
Parcere subiectis et debellare superbos.
These shall be thine arts – to impose civilisation after
peace, to spare the conquered and subdue the proud.

Heu pietas! Heu prisca fides!
Alas for piety! Alas for old time faith!

Hi motus animorum atque haec certamina tanta
Pulveris exigui iactu compressa quiescunt.
These turbulent hearts and these mighty battles are
stilled by the throwing of a little dust.
   About the bees

Hic amor, haec patria est.
Here is my love, here is my native land.

Horresco referens.
I shudder to recall it.

Incipe, parve puer, risu cognoscere matrem.
Begin, baby boy, to recognise your mother with a
smile.

Infandum, regina, iubes renovare dolorem.
Unspeakable, O queen, is the grief which you ask
me to renew.

Macte virtute.
Be strong in virtue.

Magnus ab integro saeclorum nascitur ordo. Iam redit et
Virgo, redeunt Saturnia regna, Iam nova progenies caelo
demittitur alto.
From the cycle of years a great age is born. Now returns
the virgin godess, now returns the reign of Saturn, now
descends a newborn race from heaven above.

Malo me Galatea petit, lasciva puella,
Et fugit ad salices et se cupit ante videri.
Galatea, mischievous girl, throws an apple at me, and
flees into the willows and wants me to see where she
goes.

Manet alta mente repostum
Iudicium Paridis spretaeque iniuria formae.
Deep in her heart lie the judgement of Paris and the
insult of her slighted beauty.

Manibus date lilia plenis.
Give me lilies by the armful.

Mirabile dictu.
Wondrous to relate.

Monstrum, horrendum, informe, ingens.
A monster, horrible, misshapen, huge.
> *Of the Cyclops Polyphemus*

Non tali auxilio nec defensoribus istis.
This is not the kind of help nor are those the
champions that we need.

Nulla salus bello.
There's no safety in war.

Numeros memini, si verba tenerem.
I'd remember the tune if only I could get the words.

O fortunati nimium, sua si bona norint, Agricolae.
O happy farmers, if only they recognised their own good fortune!

O mihi praeteritos referat si Iuppiter annos!
Oh that Jupiter would give me back the years that are past!

O passi graviora, dabit deus his quoque finem!
O you who have suffered worse, God will bring an end to this too.

Obstupui, steteruntque comae et vox faucibus haesit.
I was astounded, my hair stood on end and my voice stuck in my throat.

Omnia vincit amor, nos et cedamus amori.
Love conquers all; let us yield to love.

Penitus toto divisos orbe Britannos.
Britons, virtually separated from the whole world.

Per varios casus, per tot discrimina rerum, Tendimus in Latium.
Through many chances and changes of fortune we press on towards Latium.

Possunt quia posse videntur.
They can because it's thought they can.

Primo avulso non deficit alter
Aureus, et simili frondescit virga metallo.
When a bough is torn away, another golden bough
grows with leaves of the same metal.

Procul, o procul este, profani.
Away, away, ye profane.

Quadrupedante putrem sonitu quatit ungula campum.
With four-footed pulse the hoof shakes the dusty
plain.
   An example of onomatopoeia

Qui amant ipsi sibi somnia fingunt.
Lovers construct their own dreams.

Rari nantes in gurgite vasto
Scattered swimmers in the huge sea.

Regum aequabat opes animis; seraque revertens
Nocte domum, dapibus mensas onerabat inemptis.
In his heart he equalled the wealth of kings; returning
home at night, he loaded his table with unbought
feasts.
   About a happy old man who cultivates his garden

Sed fugit interea, fugit inreparabile tempus.
But time flies, irretrievable time.

Si parva licet componere magnis.
If one may compare small things with great.

Sic itur ad astra.
This is the way to the stars.

Stat sua cuique dies; breve et irreparabile tempus
Omnibus est vitae; sed famam extendere facti,
Hoc virtutis opus.
Every man has his appointed day; to all men a short
and unalterable span of life; but by deeds to extend
our fame, this is virtue's task.

Sunt geminae Somni portae, quarum altera fertur
Cornea, qua veris facilis datur exitus umbris,
Altera candenti perfecta nitens elephanto,
Sed falsa ad caelum mittunt insomnia Manes.
There are twin gates of Sleep, one said to be of horn
through which true ghosts may readily pass, the other
wrought of shining ivory but through it the spirits send
false dreams up to the world.

Sunt lacrimae rerum et mentem mortalia tangunt.
Tears are due and the fate of mortal man touches the
heart.

Tacitum vivit sub pectore vulnus.
The wound festers silently within his breast.

Tantae molis erat Romanam condere gentem.
So huge was the effort to found the Roman race.

Tendebantque manus ripae ulterioris amore.
They stretched out their hands in longing for the
further shore.

Terra antiqua, potens armis atque ubere glebae.
An ancient land, strong in arms and in the richness of the soil.

Timeo Danaos et dona ferentes.
I fear the Greeks, even [or especially] when they bear gifts.

Tityre, tu patulae recubans sub tegmine fagi
Silvestrem tenui Musam meditaris avena.
Tityrus, lying beneath a roof of spreading beech, you practice a woodland Muse upon your slim reed.

Tot congesta manu praeruptis oppida saxis
Fluminaque antiquos subterlabentia muros.
So many towns piled on steep crags by the hands of men, and rivers flowing beneath ancient walls.

Tuta timens.
Frightened even when there is no danger.

Ultima Thule.
Furthest Thule (*i.e.* the utmost corner of the world).

Una salus victis nullam sperare salutem.
The only safety for the conquered is to have no hope of safety.

Varium et mutabile semper
Femina
Woman, always fickle and changeable.

Vera incessu patuit dea.
You could see as she walked that she was a goddess
indeed.

Vires acquirit eundo.
She acquires strength as she goes.
  On rumour

Thomas Wolsey (c 1475-1530)
Ego et rex meus.
I and my king.
  *(Wrongly thought to be arrogant but in fact the correct
  Latin word order)*

INDEX

A

abest: Nescio quid curtae semper a rei 32
absurdum: Reduction ad a. 11
Academi: Inter silvas a. 31
Achates: Fidus A. 66
acti: Laudator temporis a. 32
actum: Nil a. credens 47
actus: A. non facit 42
adiuvat: Fortes fortuna a. 64
adolescens: Quem di diligunt a. moritur 51
aegrot: a. at daemon 2
aes: A. triplex 27
  Illi robur et a. triplex 31
aestimes: A. iudicia, non numeres 44
aeternam: Requiem a. dona eis 59
aeternitatis: Sub specie a. 61
afflavit: A. Deus et dissipantur 2
Africa: Ex A. semper aliquid novi 52
Agamemnona: Vixere fortes ante A. 40
agendum: quid superesset a. 47
  agnus: A. Dei, miserere nobis 56
Agricolae: sua si bona norint, A. 71
alea: Iacta a. est 31
alia: Inter a. 7
alienum: humani a me a. puto 64
aliter: Dis a. visum 67
alma: A. mater 2
alteram: Audi a. partem 16
altos: Vita hominum a. ressus 52
amant: qui a. ipsi sibi somnia fingunt 72
amantium: A. irae amoris integratio 63
amantum: periuria ridet a. 50
amare: A. et sapere vis deo conceditur 44
amari: Surgit a. aliquid 5
amat: Qui me a., a. et canem meum 47
amavi: Sero te a., pulchritudo 18
ambulando: Solvitur a. 12
amet: Cras a. qui nunquam amavit 51
amo: Odi et a. 20
amor: Hic a., haec patria est 69
  Omnia vincit a. 71
amori: nos et cedamus a. 71
amoris: Amantium irae a. integratio 63
amorum: Age iam meorum Finis a. 27
amphora: A. coepit 27
Angli: Non A. sed angeli 27
anguilla: A. est 51
angulus: mihi praeter omnes A. ridet 30

animae: a. naturaliter Christianae! 65
animula: A., vagula, blandula 27
animum: Caelum non a. mutant 28
annuncio: A. vobis gaudium magnum 56
ante: Status quo a. bellum 13
antiqua: Terra a. 74
antiquas: Stare super a. vias 60
apes: Ubi mel ibi a. 42
Apollo: Sic me servavit A. 39
  Neque semper arcum Tendit A. 34
apparatus: Persicos odi, puer, a. 37
aras: Usque ad a. 15
arbiter: A. elegantiae 51
Arcades: A. ambo 66
Arcadia: Et ego in A. 4
ardua: Per a. ad astra 10
arduis: Aequam memento rebus in a. 27
Argos: Dulcis moriens reminiscitur A. 67
arma: Silent leges inter a. 23
ars: A. est celare artem 2
  A.longa, vita brevis 27
  Omnis a. imitatio est naturae 61
artifex: Qualis a. pereo 49
Arrius: Dicere et insidias A. 20
asinorum: Pons a. 54
assentior: Dum lego, a. 22
astra: Sic itur ad a. 73
  Per ardua ad a. 10
Athenas: Ululas A. portas 55
Atticum: Sal A. 12
audi: A. alterem parte 16
auditorem: ad notas a. rapit 38
auxilium: Post bellum a. 54
ave: frater, a. atque vale 20
Averno: Facilis descensus A. 67
avulso: Primo a. non deficit alter 72
avis: Rara a. 50

B

Bandusiae: O fons B. 36
beatum: Nihil est ab omni Parte b. 34
beatus: B. ille, qui procul negotiis 28
bello: Nulla salus b. 70
bellum: Status quo ante b. 13
bibendum: Nunc est b. 35
bombinans: Chimaera b. in vacuo 56
bono: Cui b. 22

bonum: Summum b. 24
brevis: B. esse laboro 28
Britannos: Penitus toto divisos orbe B. 71
Brute: Et tu, B! 41
Brutum: B. fulmen 3

C

caelo: C. tonantem 28
caelum: C. non animum mutant 28
Caesar: Ave, C., morituri te salutant 2
   Aut C. aut nullus 41
calami: Lapsus c. 8
calamo: Currente c. 5
calumniare: Audacter c. semper aliquid 19
canem: Cave c. 51
   amat et c. meum 54
canere: Palinodum c. 61
candida: C. me capiet 49
canis: latrat statim et alter c. 53
cano: Arma virumque c. 66
cantate: C. Domino 56
capax: Omnium consensu c. imperii 63
carere: crimine iudico c. oportere 42
carmina: cuius c. nemo legit 48
carpe: C. diem 39
Carthago: Delenda est C. 19
casitatem: Da mihi c. et continentiam 16
Cato: C.mirari se aiebat 21
Catoni: sed victa C. 47
Catonis: Narratur et prisci C. 33
catus: C amat pisces 3
causa: Roma locuta est, c. finita est 17
caute: Nisi caste, saltem c. 53
cave: C. canem 51
caveat: C. emptor 44
cedamus: nos et c.amori 71
celare: Ars est c. artem 2
Cerere: Sine C. et Libero 64
certum: C. est quia impossible 65
cervicem: Romanus unam c. haberet 19
chimaera: C. bombinas in vacuo 56
Christianae: animae naturaliter C. 65
circenses: Panem et c. 43
circumspice: Si monumentum
   requiris, c. 12
cito: Bis dat qui c. dat 1
civis: C. Romanus sum 21
civitas: Magna c., magna solitudo 8
cogito: C. ergo sum 1
cognoscere: risu c. matrem 68
   Felix qui potuit rerum c. causas 68

coitum: Omne animal post c. triste 54
comitatus: Posse c. 10
componere: Si parva licet c. magni 72
compos: Non c. mentis 9
confundar: non c. in aeternum 58
coniugum: c. ut bonis bona 64
consensu: Omnium c. capax imperii 63
Consule: C. Planco 35
conturbat: Timor mortis c. me 26
cor: Fecisti nos ad te et inquietum
   est c. 17
corda: Sursum c. 60
Corinthum: homini contingit adire C. 34
coronat: Finis c. opus 53
corruptissima: C. in republica
   plurimae leges 62
corpus: Habeas c. 44
corruptio: c. optimi pessima 3
crambe: c. repetita magistris 43
cras: C.ingens iterabimus aequor 29
creditum: quod ab omnibus c. est 66
credo: C. ut intelligam 1
credula: quam minime c. postero 39
credulus: Qui nunc te fruitur c. aurea 30
crepidam: Ne sutur ultra c. 16
cucullus: c. non facit monachum 3
cui: C. bono? 22
culpa: Mea c., mea maxima c. 58
cunctando: nobis c. resituit rem 26
Cupidinesque: Lugete, O Veneres C. 20
curtae: nescio quid c. semper abest
   rei 34
custodes: sed quis custodiet ipsos C. 43
cygno: nigroque simillima c. 50
Cynarae: bonae sub regno C. 35

D

daemon: Aegrot at d. monachus 2
damnosa: D. hereditas 26
Danaos: Timeo D. et dona ferentes 74
dapibus: d. mensas onerabat inemptis 72
David: Teste D. cum Sybilla 65
dea: Vera incessu patuit d. 75
decipi: Populus vult d. 19
decus: D. et tutamen 67
defensor: Fidei D. 57
delenda: D. est Cathago 19
deliberamus: Dum d. quando
   incipiendum 55
delicto: In flagrante d. 44
dementat: deus vult perdere prius d. 54

demonstrandum: Quod erat d. 11
Deo: D. optimo maximo 56
 D. volente 57
deos: Expedit esse d., e, ut expedit 49
 d. flebit et aspera 32
desiderio: Quis d. sit pudor aut
 modus 38
desipere: Dulce est d. in loco 33
desperandum: Nil d. Teucro 34
desunt: Cetera d. 3
deteriora: D. sequor 50
Deum: et hoc omnes intelligunt D. 16
 O noctes cenaeque deum 36
 Te D. laudamus 1
 deus: Afflavit D. et dissipantus 2
 D. ex machina 57
 dabit d. his quoque finem 71
 Quem d. vult perdere 54
 Vae! Puto d. fio 66
 Homo proponit, sed D. disponit 1
dicebamus: D. hesterno die... 25
dictu: Mirabile d. 70
dictum: D. sapienti sat est 51
 Obiter d. 10
die: Sine d. 46
diem: Carpe d. 39
 Amici, d. perdidi 65
dies: D irae, d. illa 65
 Stat sua cuique d. 73
digito: At pulchrum est d. monstrari 50
dignitatem: Infra d. 7
dilige: D. et quod vis fact 17
dimittis: Nunc d. 59
dis: D. aliter visum 67
disponit: Homo proponit, sed Deus d. 1
disputandum: De gustibus non d. 4
dissipantur: Afflavit Deus et d. 2
divide: D. et impera 4
divisa: Gallia est omnis d. in partes
 tres 41
dixerunt: ante nos nostra d. 41
dolorem: regina, iubes renovare d. 69
doloris: socios habuisse d. 12
dolorosa: Stabat Mater d. 25
domina: Emax d. 49
Domine: In te, D., speravi:
 Non nobis, D. 58
 Requiem aeternam dona eis, D. 59
Domino: Cantate Domino 56
Dominus: D. vobiscum 57
dona: Timeo Danaos et d. ferentes 74

dormienda: Nox est perpetua una d. 20
duelli: d. paenitet 42
dulce: D. est desipere in loco 33
 D. et decorum est 29
 D. ridentem Lalagen amabo 29
durum: D! Sed levius fit patientia 29

E

ecclesiam: Salus extra e. non est 17
edax: Tempus e. rerum 39
ego: E. et rex meus 75
elabitur: Anguilla est, e. 51
elegantiae: Arbiter e. 62
elenchi: Ignorantia e. 6
emax: E. domina 49
emptor: Caveat e. 44
entia: E. non sunt multiplicanda 49
epicuri: E. de grege porcum 30
episcopari: Nolo e. 59
equitem: Post e. 37
ergo: Post hoc, e. propter hoc 11
 Cogito, e. sum 25
errare: E. humanum est 25
error: Mentis gratissimus e. 32
erupit: Abiit, excessit, evasit, e. 21
esse: E. oportet ut vivas 22
Etona: Floreat E. 5
eundo: Vires acquirit e. 75
evasit: Abiit, excessit, e. erupit 21
excrucior: Nescio: sed fieri sentio, et e. 20
experimentum: Fiate e. corpore vili 5
exeunt: E. omnes 5

F

fabula: Mutato nomone de te F. narratur
 33
fac: Dilige et quod vis f. 17
facit: f. indignatio versum 43
falsi: Suggestio f., suppressio veri 13
fato: Nemo fit f. nocens 61
favete: F. linguis 30
felicitas: Curiosa f. 51
felix: F. qui potuit rerum cognoscere
 causas 68
femina: Dux f. facti 67
 in qua non f. litem moverit 43
 Varium et mutabile semper F. 74
festina: f. lentes 16
fidei: F. Defensor 57
fidem: Heu quotiens fidem 30
fides: Heu pietas! Heu prisca f. 69

Uberrima f. 46
fidus: F. Achates 68
filiam: vertatem temporis f. esse dixit 18
finis: F. coronat opus 53
  Age iam meorum F. amorum 27
flagrante: In f. delicto 46
flammae: Agnosco veteris vestigia f. 66
flava: capiet me f. puella 49
fons: O f. Bandusiae 36
  F. et origo 5
fonte: Medio de f. leporum 47
formae: spretaeque iniuria f. 70
fortes: F. fortunat adiuvat 64
  Vixere f. ante Agamemnona 40
fortiter: Suaviter in mondo, f.in re 13
fortuna: F. vitrea est 55
Fortes f. adiuvat 64
  Stat f. domus 68
fortunatam: O f. natam, me consule, 23
frigida: Pallidula, f., nudula 27
frugiferi: Agri non omnes f. sunt 21
fugit: f. interea, f. inreparabile tempus 72
fulmen: Brutum f. 3
furca: naturam expelles f. 37

G

Galatea: Malo me Galatea petit 70
Galilaee: Vicisti G. 41
galeatum: G. sero duelli paenitet 42
gaudeamus: G. igitu 6
generis: Sui g. 14
genius: G. loci 6
genus: Et hoc g. omne 30
  G. immortale manet 68
gesserit: Dum se bene g. 44
gladius: In eburna vagina plumbeus g. 25
gloria: Militavi non sine gloria 33
  sic transit g. mundi 59
Gotham: Veni G., ubi multos 25
Graecum: G. est 6
gratissimus: Mentis g. error 6
gratum: Nihil aeque g. est adeptis 52
gustibus: De g. non disputandum 4

H

haruspex: non rideret h. haruspicem 21
Herculem: Ex pede H. 5
hereditas: Damnosa h. 26
Homerus: dormitat H. 31
hominum: Vita h. altos 52
homo: Ecce h! 52, 57

Novus h. 10
H. proponit 1
horas: H. non numero nisi serenas 6
horrendum: Monstrum, h. 70
horresco: H. referens 69
hostis: Pirata est h. humani generis 24
humani: h. nil a me alienum puto 64
humaniores: Literae h. 8
humanum: Errare h. est 25

I

iacta: I. alea est 41
Iesus: I. Nazarenus Rex Iudaeorum 58
ignotius: Ignotum per i. 6
ignotum: Omne i. pro magnifico 63
Ilium: Fuit I. 68
imitatio: Omnis ars i. est naturae 61
impavidum: i. ferient ruinae 38
impera: Divide et i. 4
imperii: Omnium consensu capax i. 63
impossibile: Certum est quia i 65
impune: Nemo me i. lacessit 9
incognita: Terra i. 14
indecora: Intuta quae i. 63
indefensi: Inauditi atque i. 62
indignatio: facit i. versum 43
  Saeva i. 12
indignor: I. quandoque bonus dormitat
    Homerus 31
inemptis: dapibus mensas onerabat i. 72
infandum: I., regina, iubes renovare
    dolorem 69
infidelium: In partibus i. 58
informe: Monstrum, horrendum, i., 70
infra: I. dignitatem 7
ignotum: Omne i. pro magnifico 63
  I. per ignotius 6
iniuria: Summum ius summa i. 24
  spretaeque i. formae 70
  Volenti non fit i. 46
iniuratam: mantem i. gero 22
innocentes: tamquam i. perierant 62
inops: Magnas inter opes i. 32
inquietum: Fecisti nos ad te et i. est 17
intelligam: Credo ut i. 1
intentata: Miseri, quibus I. nites 33
inter: Primus i. pares 11
intuta: I. quae indecora 63
Iovem: credimus I. regnare 28
Iovi: Quod licet I. no licet bovi 55
irae: Dies i, dies illa 65

ite: I., missa est 58
iudicat: Securus i. orbis tarrarum 18
iudicata: Res i. 46
iudice: Me i. 8
iudicia: Aestimes i. non numeres 44
Iuppiter: I. ex alto periuria ridet
amantum 50
referat si I. annos 71
iurare: i. in verba magistri 35
iurari: i. lingua 22
ius: Summum i. summa iniuria 24
iustitia: Fiat i. 26
iustitiae: sine ulla particula i. vivere 22
iustitiam: nulli deferemus i. 46
iustum: I. et tenacem propositi virum 32
iuvabit: haec olim memnisse i. 68
iuvenes: Gaudeamus igitur I. 6

J

judice: Sub j. 46

K

kalendas: ad K. Graecas solutoros 61

L

labor: Hic opus, hic l.est 67
laborare: L. est orare 53
laborem: magnum alterius spectare l. 48
lacessit: Nemo me impune l. 9
lacrimae: Hinc illae l. 31
Sunt l. rerum 73
Lalagen: Duclce ridentem L. amabo 29
lapsus: L. clami 8
lares: L. et penates 8
lasciva: Malo me Galatea petit, l. puella 70
Latinum: Tendimus in L. 71
latrante: L. uno, latrat statim et alter
canis 53
Prospectandum vetulo l. 54
laudamus: Te Deum l. 1
laudator: L. temporis acti 32
lavat: Manus manum l. 61
lege: Tolle l. 18
Servata semper l. 43
leges: Silent l. inter arma 26
Iudicium parium aut l. terrae 44
Corruptissima in republica
plurimae l. 62
legi: Graecum est. Non potest l. 6
legiones: Vare, redde l. 16
lego: Dum l, assentior 22

lente: Festina l. 16
Lesbia: Vivamus, mea L. 21
lex: L. talionis 45
De minimis non curat l. 24
libelli: Habent sua fata l. 65
Libero: Sine Cerere et L. 64
Libitinam: mei vitabit L. 35
libri: Timeo homienem unius l. 18
lilia: Manibus date l. plenis: 70
linguis: Favete l. 30
literae: L. humaniores 8
loci: Genius l. 6
loco: Dulce eet desipere in l. 35
locum: L. tenens 45
locus: L. paenitentiae 45
loquendi: et ratione l. 43
...ius et norma l. 39
loquitur: Res ipsa l. 46
lucas: L. a non lucendo 55
lucendo: Lucus a non l. 55
lucernam: Olet l. 54
luna: Velut inter ignes L. minores 40
lux: Fiat l. 57

M

machina: Deus ex m. 57
macte: M. virtute 69
magna: m. civitas, m. solitudo 8
maiorum: More m. 9
malo: m. m. m. m. 8
M. cum Platone 22
M. me Galatea petit 70
malum: M. in se. M. prohibitum 45
mandamus: 45
mansuetae: M. naturae 45
manus: M. manum lavat 61
Tendebantque m. ripae 73
mare: qui trans m. currunt 28
marmoream: gloriatus m. se relinquere 62
mater: Alma m. 2
Stabat M. dolorosa 25
matrem: risu cognoscere m. 69
Mauris: non eget M. iaculis 31
maximo: Deo optimo m. 56
medias: in m. res 38
mediocritatem: Auream quisquis m. 28
meliora: Video m. proboque 50
mens: M. sana in corpore sano 42
Momento: M. mori 9
memini: Numeros m.. 70
meminisse: olim m. iuvabit 68

memoria: m. rerum nostrarum 23
mendax: Splendide m. 39
mens: reum nisi m. sit rea 42
mentem: m. iniuratam gero 22
mentis: Non compos m. 9
   m. gratissimus error 32
meruit: Quantum m. 46
metuant: Oderint dum m. 62
militavi: M. non sine gloria 33
mirabile: M. dictu 70
miseri: M., quibus 33
misericordia: M. domini inter pontem 17
misereri: Agnus Dei, m. nobis 56
   M. est tacere cogi 55
missa: Ite, m. est 58
   Nescit vox m. reverti 34
mobilium: M. turba Quiritium 33
modus: M. vivendi 9
monachum: Cucullus non facit m. 3
monachus: m. tunc esse volebat 2
monstrare: Nequo m. 43
   monstrum: M., horrendum, 70
monumetum: Exegi m. aere perennius 30
   Si m. requiris, circumspice 12
mora: Maximum remedium irae m. est 22
more: m. maiorum 9
mores: O tempora! O m! 23
   Abeunt studia in m. 49
mori: pro patria m. 29
moriens: Dulcis m. reminisciitur Argos 67
moritur: diligunt adolescens m. 51
morituri: Ave, Caesar, m. te salutant 3
mors: Pallida m. aequo pulsat pede 36
morti: Afferet indomitaeque m. 29
mortis: Timor m. conturbat me 26
mortuis: De m. nil nisi bonum 4
mortuus: Passer m. est meae puellae 20
moveri: Quieta non m. 54
multaque: m. pars mei Vitabit Libitinam 35
multiplicanda: Entia non sunt m. 49
munditiis: Simplex m. 39
musam: M. meditaris avena 74
mutabile: Varium et m. semper Femina 74
mutantur: Tempora m. nos et m. in illis 47

natura: n. abhorrat vacuum 25
naturae: Omnis ars imitatio est n. 61
   Mansuetae n. 45
naturam: N. expelles furca 34
natus: Nescire quod antea quam natus 23
Nazarenus: Iesus N. Rex Iudaeorum 58
nigroque: n. simillima cygno 50
nihil: Ex nihilo n. fit 47
   multa agendo n. agens 51
   N. simile est idem 9
nihilo: De n. nihil 50
nites: Misseri, quibus Intenta n. 33
nives: Diffugere n. 29
nobis: Non n. Domine 59
noctes: O n. cenaeque deum 36
noctis: Ius primae n. 7
nocturna: N. versate manu 34
nonumque: N. prematur in annum 35
nostrarum: memoria rerum n. 23
novus: N. homo 10
nox: N. est perpetua una dormienda 20
nullius: Res n. 46
numero: Hores non n. nisi serenas 6
numeros: N. memini 70
nunc: N. dimittis 59

O

obiter: O. dictum 10
obsequium: O. amicos 64
obscurus: Brevis ess elaboro, O. fio 28
obstupui: O., steteruntque comae 71
oderint: O. dum metuant 19, 23
odi: O. et amo 20
odisse: o. quem laeseris 63
odium: O. scholasticum 10
officio: Functus o. 5
olet: non o. 66
omen: Absit o. 2
omnnes: Exeunt o. 5
   O si sic o. 43
optimi: Corruptio o. pessima 3
optimo: Deo o. maximo 56
opus: Finis coronat o. 53
   hic o., hic labor est 67
orare: Laborare est o. 53
orbi: Urbi et o. 60
origo: Fons et o. 5
omavit: Nullum quod tetigit non o. 41
otiosum: Numquam se minus

N

nantes: Rari n. in gurgite vasto 72

otiosum 23
otium: Cum dignitate o. 22
ovis: O. ovem sequitur 54
ovo: bellum Troianum oritur ab o. 34
  Ab o. usque ad mala 53

P

pace: Requiescat in p. 60
pacem: Qui desiderat p. 26
  Solitudinem faciunt, p. appellant 53
pacique: P. imponere morem 68
paenitentiae: Locus p. 45
paenitet: Galeatum sero duelli p. 42
pallida: P. mors aequo pulsat 36
papam: Habemus p. 56
paratos: O hominess ad servitutem p. 63
parce: P., precor, precor 31
parentis: In loco p. 7
paribus: Ceteris p. 3
Paridis: p. spretaeque iniuria formae 45
parmula: Relicta non bene P. 38
Parnassum: Gradus ad p. 30
particula: sine ulla p. iustitiae vivere 7
parturiunt: P. montes 36
parva: Si p. licet componere magnis 72
parvo: Multum in p. 9
passi: O p. graviora 71
paterna: P rura bobus exercet suis 28
patientia: Durum! Sed levius fit p. 29
partia: pro p. mori 29
  Hic amor, haec p. est 69
pauciora: quod potest fieri per p. 49
pauperis: In forma p. 44
pax: P. vobiscum 59
peccator: Esto p. et pecca 48
pecatore: In p. 50
penates: Lares et p. 8
penitus: P toto divisos orbe Britannos 71
perdidi: Amici, diem p. 65
pereant: P. illi qui ante nos nostra
                dixerunt 41
perennius: Exegi monumentum aere p. 30
periuria: Iuppiter ex alto p. 50
perpetua: Esto p. 61
  Nox est p. una dormienda 20
persicos: P. odi 37
pessima: Corruptio optimi p. 3
petitio: P. principii 10
pictura: Animum p. pascit imani 66
pietas: Heu p! Heu prisca fides 69
pirata: P. est hostis humani generis 24

pisces: Catus amat p. 3
Planco: Consule p. 35
Plato: Amicus P. 21
Platone: Malo cum P. errare 22
plaudite: Vos valete et p. 65
plaudo: at mihi p. 36
plebis: venor suffragia p. 3
plumbeus: In eburna vagina p. gladius 3
plura: Frustra fit per p. 49
pluribus: E p. unum 67
pocula: Inter p. 7
pollice: P. verso 10
pons: P. asinorum 54
pontem: Misericordia domini inter p. 17
populus: P. me sibilat 37
  P. vult decipi 19
populusque: Senatus P. Romanus 11
porcum: Epicuri de grege p. 30
posse: p. comitatus 10
possidetis: Uti p. 15
possum: Hoc tantum p. dicere 48
possunt: P. quia posse videntur 71
post: P. bellum auxilium 54
  P. hoc 11
posteri: Credite p. 29
postume: Eheu! Fugaces, p. 29
potens: Terra antique, p. armis 74
potestas: Ipsa scientia p. est 19
praeteritos: O mihi p. referat si
                Iuppiter 71
prematur: Nonumque p. in annum 35
primae: Ius p. noctis 7
primum: ad aliquod p. movens 16
primus: P inter pares 31
procul: P., o. p. este, profani 72
profani: Procul, o, procul este, p. 72
profanum: Odi p. vulgus et arceo 36
profundis: de p. clamavi ad te, Domine 56
prohibitum: Malum in se, Malum p. 45
prosequi: Nolle p. 45
prospectandum: P. veulo latrante 54
prudenter: p. agis et respice finem 11
puella: capiet me flava p. 49
  Malo me Galatea petit, lasciva p. 3
puellarum: Quem si p. insereres choro 37
pulchritudo: p. tam antique 18
pulchrum: At p. est digito monstrari 50
pulveris: P. exigui iactu compressa 69
pulvis: P et umbra sumus 37
pupillari: In statu p. 6
purus: Integer vitae scelerisque p. 31

purpureus: P. late qui splendeat unus et
alter 37

Q

quadrupedante: Q. putrem sonitu 72
quantula: Nescis, mi fili, q. sapientia 50
quantum: Q. meruit 46
  Q. sufficit 11
quiatat: Mente sq. solida 33
quieta: Q. non moveri 54
quod: Q. erat demonstrandum 11
quoque: Tu q. 14

R

rara: R. avis 50
rasa: Tabula r. 14
ratio: Ultima r. regum 15
ratione: semper lege et r. loquendi 43
rea: Actus non facit reum nisi mens
sit r. 42
rebus: Aequam memento r. in arduis 27
redit: Iam r. et Virgo 69
reductio: R. ad absurdum 11
referens: Horresco r. 69
refero: Relata r. 10
regina: Infandum, r., iubes renovare 63
regnare: Caelo tonantem credimus
Iovem r.
28
regum: R. aequabat opes animis 72
  Ultima ratio r. 15
relata: R. refero 11
religientum: R. esse oportet, religiosum
nefas 18
relinquere: gloriatus marmoream se r. 62
rem: qui r. facias, r. 26
remedium: Maximum r. 22
renovare: iubes r. dolorem 69
requiem: R. aeternam dona eis 59
requescat: R. in pace 60
res: R. ipsa loquitur 46
  R. iudicata 46
  R. nullius 46
respice: prudenter agis et r. finem 11
retosum: adversum spectantia, nulla r. 40
retro: Vador r., Satana 60
retrorsum: nunc r. Vela dare 36
rex: Ego et r. meus 75
ridentem: Quamquam r. dicere verum 37
ridiculus: nascetur r. mus 36
risus: Sardonius r. 12

Roma: R. locuta est 17
Romam: me consule, R. 23
Romanam: Tantae molis erat R. 73
Romanis: Intoleeranda R. vox 47
Romanus: Civil R. sum 21
  R. unam cervicem haberet 19
  Senatus Populusque R. 13
  Utinam populus R. 19
rosa: Sub r. 13
rotundus: Teres atque r. 40
rumoresque: R. senum severiorum 21
rus: R. in urbe 48

S

sabbata: O quanta qualia sunt illa s. 1
Sabidi: Non amo te, S. 48
sal: S.Atticum 12
salis: Addito s. grano 52
  Cum grano s. 3
salus: Nulla s. bello 70
  S. extra ecclesiam non est 17
  Una s. victis 74
sana: Mens s. in corpore sano 42
sancta: O s. simplicitas 40
sapere: Amare et s. vix deo conceditur 44
sapienti: Verbus s. sat est 51
  Dictum s. sat est 64
sapientia: Nescis, mi fili, quantula s. 50
Sardonius: S. risus 12
Satana: Vade retro, S. 60
scelerisque: Integer vitae s. purus 31
scenam: Digna geri promes in s. 35
scholasticum: Odium s. 10
scientia: Ipsa s. potestas est 19
scio: Si nemo ex me quaerat, s; 17
scribendi: s. cacoethes 44
scribit: Non s., cuius carmina 48
scyphis: Natis in usum laetitia s. 33
Senatus: S. Populusque Romanus 13
sententiae: Quot homines tot s. 64
sentio: Nequeo monstrare, et s. tantum 43
serenas: Horas non numero nisi s. 6
servavit: Sic me s. Apollo 39
servitutem: O hominess ad s. paratos 63
sesquipedelia: S. verba 38
sibilat: Populus me s. 37
sidera: Sublimi feriam s. vertice 39
signo: In hoc s. vinces 7
silent: S. leges inter arma 23
silvas: Inter s. Academi 31
silvestrem: S. tenui Musam 74

simile: Nihil s. est idem 9
simplex: S. munditiis 39
simplicitas: O sancta s. 40
sine: S. die 46
  S. qua non 12
Sirmio: Paene insularum, S. 20
Socrates: amicus s. 21
solamen: S. miseris socios 12
solida: Mente quatit s. 32
solitudo: Magna civitas, magna s. 8
solitudinem: S. faciunt, pacem appellant 63
solum: Cuius est s. 24
  nec minus s. 23
solvitur: S. ambulando 12
somni: Sunt geminae S. portae 73
somnia: qui amant ipsi sibi s. fingunt 72
Soracte: S., nec iam sustineant onus 40
specie: Sub s. aeternitatis 61
species: O quanta s. cerebrum non habet 51
spectatum: S. veniunt 50
speravi: In te, Domine, s. 58
spero: Dum spiro, s. 4
splendide: S. mendax 39
spretaeque: Paridis s. injuria formae 70
standi: Locus s. 45
stet 13
status: S. quo ante belluls 13
stomachor: S. omnia 24
studia: Abeunt s. in mores. 49
stultus: Interdum s. bene loquitur 53
suaviter: s. in modo 13
sub: S. judice 46
  S. rosa 13
subjectis: Parcere s. et debellare superbos 68
sufficit: Quantum s. 11
suffragia: venor s. plebis 35
suggestio: S. falsi 13
sum: Cogito, ergo s. 25
summum: S. bonum 24
sursum: S. corda 60
suspicione: Meos tam s. quam crimine 42
sutor: Ne s. ultra crepidam 16
Sybilla: Teste David cum S. 65

T

taberna: in t. mori 48

tabula: T rasa 14
taedium: T. vitae 14
tacere: Misere est t. 55
tacitum: T. vivit sub pectore vulnus 73
tali: Non t. auxilio 70
talonis: Lex t. 45
tangere: Noli me t. 59
tempora: T. mutantur 47
  O t! O mores! 23
temporis: veritatem t. filiam esse dixit 18
  Laudator t. acti 32
tempus: T. edax rerum 39
  Quid est ergo t. 17
  fugit inreparabile t. 72
tendebantque: T. manus 73
tendimus: T. in Latium 71
tenens: Locum t. 45
terminus: T. a quo 14
terra: T. antique, ptens armis 74
T. incognita 14
tertium: T. quid 14
tetigisti: Rem acu t. 52
Teucro: Nil desperandum T. duce 34
theologicum: Odium t. 10
Thracum: Pugnare T. est 33
Thule: Ultima T. 74
timens: Tuta t. 74
timeo: T. hominem unius libri 18
Tite: O T. tute Tati tibi tanta 26
Tityre: T., tu patulae recubans 74
Traiani: Imperium T. 62
transit: sic t. gloria mundi 59
triplex: Aes t. 27
triste: Omne animal post coitum t. 54
Troianum: Nec gemino bellum T. 34
tuba: At t. terribili sonitu taratantara 26
  T. mirum spargens sonum 60
turba: Mobilium t. Quiritium 33
tuta: T. timens 74
tutamen: Decus et t. 67
tutissimus: In medio t. ibis 49
tyrannis: Sic semper t. 19

U

urbi: U. et orbi 60
ubique: Quod u., quod semper 66
ultima: U. ratio regum 15
  U. thule 74
umbra: Magnus nominis u. 47
  Pulvis et u. sumus 37

ungula: sonitu quatit u. campum 72
unum: E pluribus u. 67
urbe: Rus in u. 48
urceus: currente rota cur u. exit 28
usus: Si volet u. 39

V

vacuum: Natura abhorrat v. 25
vacuus: Cantabit v. 42
vade: V. mecum 15
 V. retro, Satana. 60
vadis: Quo v? 59
vae: Intoleranda Romanis vox, V. victis 47
vale: In perpetuum, frater, ave atque v. 20
valent: Tantum bona v. 24
valete: Vos v. et plaudite 65
vanitas: V. vanitatum 60
vare: V. redde legiones 16
varium: V et mutabile semper Femina 74
vas: Malum v. non frangitur 53
veni, v., vidi, vici 42
 V. Gotham 25
veniunt: Spectatum v., v. spectentur e 50
venus: Itermissa, V, diu rursus bella 31
 Sine Cerere et Libero frigit v. 64
verba: Ipsissima v. 7
 Numeros memini, si v. tenerem 70
 Sesquipedelia v. 38
verborum: tum maxime v. est 1
veri: Suggestio falsi, supressio v. 13
veritas: In vino v. 53
 Magna est v. et praevalet 58
 v. odium parit 64
 sed magis amica v. 21
veritatem: v. temporis filiam 18
versa: vice v. 15
versate: Nocturna v. manu, v. diurna 34
vestigia: Agnosco veteris v. flammae 66
vetulo: Prospectandum v. latrante 54
vias: Stare super antiquas v. 60
viator: Cantabit vacuus coram latrone v. 42

vicisti: V. Galilaee 41
victis: Una salus v. 74
 Intoleranda Romanis vox, Vae v. 47
victrix: V. causas deis placuit 47
videlicet: V. 15
video: V. meliora proboque 50
vidi: Veni, v., vici 42
vinces: In hoc signo v. 7
vincit: Omnia v. amor 71
vino: In v. veritas 53
Virgilianae: Sortes V. 13
Virgo: Iam redit et V. 69
virtus: Saepe mero caluisse v. 33
virtute: Macte v. 69
virtutem: Disce, puer, v. ex me 67
virtutis: Hoc v. opus 73
vita: V. hominum altos recessus 52
 Ars longa, v. brevis 27
vitae: V. summa brevis 36
 Taedium v. 14
vitrea: Fortuna v. est 55
vivamus: Dum vivimus, v. 4
 V., mea Lesbia 21
vivendi: Modus v. 9
vivere: non v. ut edas 22
 Tecum v. amem 39
vixit 15
vobiscum: Dominus v. 57
volat: v. irrevocable verbum 38
volente: Deo v. 57
volenti: V. non fit iniuria 46
voluisse: In magnis et v. sat est 53
vox: V. et praeterea nihil 15
 V. populi, v. Dei 1
 v. faucibus haesit 71
 Nescit v. missa reverti 34
vulgus: Odi profanum v. 36
vulnus: Tacit um vivit sub pectore v. 73